ELIZEBETH FRIEDMAN

Expert Codebreaker of WORLD WAR II

by Elizabeth Pagel-Hogan   illustrated by Alisha Monnin

CAPSTONE PRESS
a capstone imprint

Published by Capstone Press, an imprint of Capstone
1710 Roe Crest Drive, North Mankato, Minnesota 56003
capstonepub.com

Library of Congress Cataloging-in-Publication Data
Names: Pagel-Hogan, Elizebeth, author. | Monnin, Alisha, illustrator.
Title: Elizebeth Friedman : expert codebreaker of World War II / by Elizebeth Pagel-Hogan ;
illustrated by Alisha Monnin. Other titles: Expert codebreaker of World War II
Description: North Mankato, Minnesota : Capstone Press, an imprint of Capstone, [2023]
| Series: Women warriors of World War II | Includes bibliographical references. | Audience:
Ages 8-11 | Audience: Grades 4-6 | Summary: "An inspiring graphic novel about Elizebeth
Friedman, a codebreaking pioneer who changed the course of World War II. Nazi spy rings!
No-good gangsters! Shakespearian lies! Discover the courageous woman who cracked all
these cases and more-with only a pencil and paper. The youngest of ten siblings, Elizebeth
Friedman stood out from an early age with brilliant language skills and a passion for English
literature. Eventually, these talents led to a new opportunity: codebreaking. Using ciphers
and other trailblazing techniques, Friedman solved coded messages to take down some
of the most notorious gangsters in the United States, including the infamous Al Capone.
During World War II, as German forces stormed across Europe, she took her skills to the
frontlines, thwarting Nazi spies and helping lead Allied forces to victory. In this action-
packed, full-color graphic novel, learn more about this daring woman who took risks, defied
expectations, and confronted the enemies of World War II"-- Provided by publisher.
Identifiers: LCCN 2023002027 (print) | LCCN 2023002028 (ebook) |
ISBN 9781669013464 (hardcover) | ISBN 9781669013419 (paperback) |
ISBN 9781669013426 (ebook pdf) | ISBN 9781669013440 (kindle edition) |
ISBN 9781669013457 (epub)
Subjects: LCSH: Friedman, Elizebeth, 1892-1980--Comic books, strips, etc.--Juvenile
literature. | World War, 1939-1945--Cryptography--Comic books, strips, etc.--Juvenile
literature. | Cryptographers--United States--Biography--Comic books, strips, etc.--Juvenile
literature. | Cryptography--United States--History--20th century--Comic books, strips, etc.-
-Juvenile literature. | Friedman, William F. (William Frederick), 1891-1969--Comic books,
strips, etc.--Juvenile literature. | World War, 1914-1918--Cryptography--Comic books,
strips, etc.--Juvenile literature.
Classification: LCC D810.C88 F77 2023 (print) | LCC D810.C88 (ebook) |
DDC 940.54/8673092 [B]--dc23/eng/20230118
LC record available at https://lccn.loc.gov/2023002027
LC ebook record available at https://lccn.loc.gov/2023002028

Editorial Credits
Editor: Donald Lemke; Designer: Sarah Bennett;
Production Specialist: Katy LaVigne

Design Elements: Shutterstock/Here

All internet sites appearing in back matter were available and accurate
when this book was sent to press.

Direct quotations appear in bold italicized text on the following pages:

TABLE OF CONTENTS

PROLOGUE: SECRETS

During World War II (1939–1945), the Nazis sent military secrets using a code they thought no one could break.

They were wrong.

The United States military had a codebreaker who uncovered their secrets and helped win the war.

Once the war was over, someone else took credit for her work and tried to hide her identity.

Elizebeth Smith Friedman knew how to make codes and break codes. And she knew *nothing stays hidden for long. Someone always uncovers secrets.*

Elizebeth Smith was born in 1892 in Huntington, Indiana. She was the youngest of 10 children.

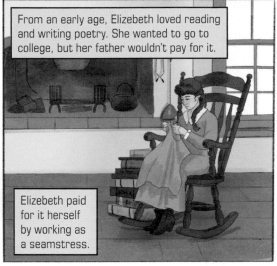

From an early age, Elizebeth loved reading and writing poetry. She wanted to go to college, but her father wouldn't pay for it.

Elizebeth paid for it herself by working as a seamstress.

After college, Elizebeth went to Chicago, Illinois, to search for a job. No one wanted to hire her.

To boost her spirits, she went to see an original copy of one of Shakespeare's plays at a nearby library.

I'm looking for a job. Something unusual.

I'll call Mr. Fabyan. He needs a college graduate who knows English literature.

George Fabyan owned a huge estate called Riverbank. He funded all kinds of scientific research, but he was most interested in one special project.

I'd like you to come and work at Riverbank.

What will I do?

You will help us find secret messages...

SOMETHING UNUSUAL

Elizebeth joined the Cipher School at Riverbank in 1916.

Mrs. Elizebeth Wells Gallup led the school and gave Elizebeth her first lesson in codes.

A good code should be easy to write and should not look like a code at all. This makes it easy to hide in plain sight.

We believe the hidden messages reveal that Sir Francis Bacon is the true author of Shakespeare's plays.

Elizebeth worked at Riverbank for four years. While there, she met William Friedman, who also worked on the Shakespeare project.

Does it seem strange that Mrs. Gallup sees messages no one else can find?

I agree. There are no hidden messages.

By 1917, Elizebeth and William wanted to leave the Shakespeare project. They had more important codes to break. The U.S. had entered World War I (1914–1918).

The essence of codebreaking is finding patterns. Let's use a frequency table.

They worked on stacks of intercepted messages from the Mexican army.

Elizebeth and William worked long hours, side by side.

I've got one here.

Double-check this will you?

They were an incredible team. In May 1917, they got married.

CODE MAKER, CODEBREAKER

In 1918, Elizebeth and William taught the first cryptology class in the country.

A code is when you use one symbol to represent another. For instance, a picture of an apple means the letter A.

A cipher is a rule for changing letters in a message.

A cipher that reverses the alphabet would change the word "apple" to "zkkov."

At the end of the course, the Friedmans and the students gathered for a class photo. The photo was, of course, a code.

Some students posed looking to the side. Others looked straight ahead. The message read: "Knowledge is Power."

After World War I ended, Elizebeth and William moved to Washington, D.C.

They had two children: a girl, Barbara, and a boy, John.

Elizebeth wanted to write books about codes. But her special skills were in demand.

Hush, Crypto!

KNOCK

RUFF! RUFF!

Mrs. Friedman? I'm Charles Root from the U.S. Coast Guard. I need your help.

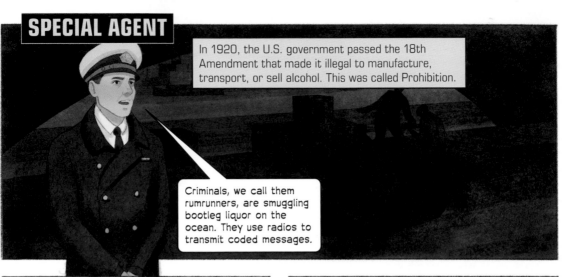

SPECIAL AGENT

In 1920, the U.S. government passed the 18th Amendment that made it illegal to manufacture, transport, or sell alcohol. This was called Prohibition.

Criminals, we call them rumrunners, are smuggling bootleg liquor on the ocean. They use radios to transmit coded messages.

We don't know what they are saying. We need you to break the codes. Will you help?

Yes, but only if I can work from home.

Elizebeth became a special agent. Once a week, she went to the treasury building and picked up a stack of coded messages.

The next week, she brought them back—solved. In her first three months of work, she solved two years' worth of coded messages.

She solved simple substitution ciphers.

She learned the names of ships carrying alcohol. She learned where and when they would anchor so agents could catch them.

She revealed the names of gangsters, business owners, and ship captains.

Elizebeth deciphered 12,000 messages in three years—all by herself.

Finally in 1931, the U.S. Treasury agreed to let her recruit a codebreaking team. She searched the lists of applicants. There were no women included, so Elizebeth hired three men.

In 1933, Elizebeth traveled to New Orleans to testify in a court case against the biggest corporation involved in rumrunning.

What is your occupation?

I am a cryptoanalyst. I analyze and read secret communications.

And your work shows that Consolidated Exporters Corporation is part of a criminal bootleg business?

Objection!

You didn't really decode secret messages. Isn't it true someone else told you these things?

No, that's not true. Your honor, if I could have a blackboard, I could explain how I solve codes.

It's an enciphered code. Words stand for letters in a cipher that stand for letters in a code.

BAM! BAM!

GUILTY!

Elizebeth helped put the criminals behind bars.

With her success in the trial and her unusual skills, Elizebeth wasn't prepared for what happened next.

She became a celebrity.

Codebreaker Cracks the Case

But Elizebeth didn't want the attention, and she didn't want to reveal her methods.

How did you crack the code?

We have to keep our ideas secret so that we do not give other smugglers any new ideas.

Elizebeth didn't like the attention. But she and William loved playing with codes. They taught their children simple ciphers. Barbara wrote coded letters home from camp.

"Dear Mother and Dear Daddy, we went on a canoe trip."

They sent holiday cards in code. Their 1928 card was a "turning grille."

People place the red paper over this grid of letters to reveal the message. They have to rotate it four times.

GERMANY

POLAND

Despite these fun games, codebreaking was Elizebeth's job. And she was about to get her most difficult assignment. World War II began on September 1, 1939, when Nazi soldiers invaded Poland.

At the beginning of the war, most Americans felt like the United States was safe. Germany was too far away to invade the U.S. directly.

It's too far for airplanes to bomb and ships are too slow.

But if the Nazis gain control of South America, they will have access to metals for machines and food for soldiers. And they would be close enough to bomb U.S. cities.

There were large German immigrant communities in South America already. Many supported Nazi fascist ideas. They wore green shirts and marched in parades.

Hitler never planned to attack South America directly. Instead, the Nazis planned a clandestine, or secret, operation. They sent in spies.

BEEP BEEP BEEP BIP BIP

In January 1940, back in Washington, D.C., Elizabeth was still decoding messages when she made a startling discovery.

Here you go.

Oh my! These aren't smugglers. They are reporting the sensitive information about the routes of U.S. and British ships to the Nazis! And the messages are coming from South America.

Before the U.S. even entered the war, spies were at work. Elizebeth spied on spies—this is called counterespionage. She was one of the first people to do this work, and it was essential that her work stayed secret.

We must crack their codes and stop them. But we cannot let them know we know.

Elizebeth relied on her tried-and-true methods. She looked for patterns and used a pencil and paper.

Can you speak German?

No, but that doesn't matter. We can look for a common German word like "zwo" that means two. The letters z and w don't occur very often in words.

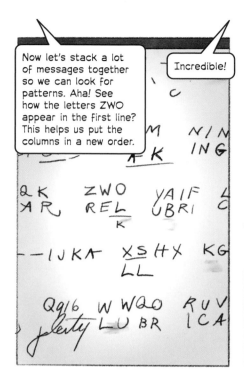

Now let's stack a lot of messages together so we can look for patterns. Aha! See how the letters ZWO appear in the first line? This helps us put the columns in a new order.

Incredible!

Elizebeth called these solved messages "decrypts." She sent her decrypts to Army and Navy intelligence. She also sent them to the Federal Bureau of Investigation, or FBI.

These decrypts are reporting on ship movements, factories that are building planes, and even changes in our politics.

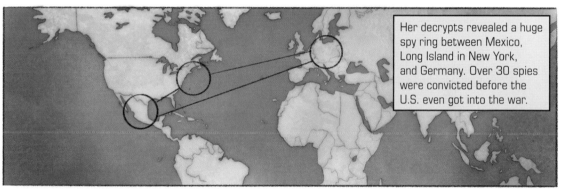

Her decrypts revealed a huge spy ring between Mexico, Long Island in New York, and Germany. Over 30 spies were convicted before the U.S. even got into the war.

The FBI exposed too much about the secret methods!

But the FBI, led by J. Edgar Hoover, took credit for all of her work. It wouldn't be the first time Elizebeth's talents were hidden. But that wasn't what really bothered her.

THE INVISIBLE WAR

After Pearl Harbor, things changed. The government didn't want civilians in charge of military operations. They appointed a Navy lieutenant to lead Elizebeth's cryptoanalyst team. But it was clear she was the one with experience.

"She is the best there is in cryptoanalysis."

Elizebeth spent three weeks helping build a cryptographic section for the new Office of Coordination of Information, which would become the OSS and CIA. But she had little faith in the man who ran this new organization.

"He treats me as a servant, but what's worse, he doesn't understand the simplest ideas of keeping information secure."

Throughout the war, both William and Elizebeth worked hard cracking codes from the enemies. But both were sworn to secrecy.

Hard day, dear?

I can't really say. You know how it is doing this spy stuff.

And things were not going to get any easier.

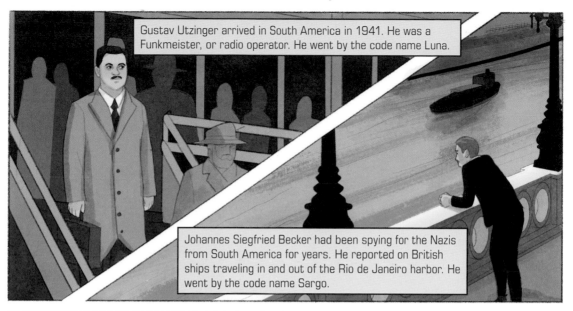

Gustav Utzinger arrived in South America in 1941. He was a Funkmeister, or radio operator. He went by the code name Luna.

Johannes Siegfried Becker had been spying for the Nazis from South America for years. He reported on British ships traveling in and out of the Rio de Janeiro harbor. He went by the code name Sargo.

Luna and Sargo were there to fight what was called the Invisible War in South America.

But Elizebeth Friedman was ready to stop them.

Elizebeth and her team worked steadily to decode the secret messages from South America.

We think they have three radio stations, two in Brazil and one in Chile on the west coast. And they are transmitting to Berlin or Hamburg.

Sargo's name appears very often in these decrypts, he must be important.

In 1942, Adolf Hitler directed the Nazis to attack U.S. and British merchant ships carrying war supplies. In three months, the U-boats sank one million tons of cargo and killed 5,000 sailors.

In March 1942, Elizebeth solved a set of messages that showed the Nazis planned to attack a ship called the *Queen Mary*, carrying almost 9,000 servicemen.

The captain must be warned!

The captain received the warnings in time and evaded the U-boat.

Then in the summer of 1942, Elizebeth learned something new and disturbing from the decoded messages.

All of these messages are full of fear and panic. They say, "Authorities in Brazil and Chile are arresting agents and seizing radios!"

Who authorized this? It's too soon to try and arrest them! These arrests will only scare the leaders deeper into hiding and they will make their codes harder to break!

At this same time, Elizebeth read messages from the spies in South America that police were hunting them down. Authorities in Brazil and Chile were arresting agents and seizing their radios.

The FBI had authorized the raids. But to really shut down the spies, the FBI needed to get all of the spies at once.

They didn't.

Sargo and Luna escaped. The Nazis changed their codes. We will have to work even harder to break them.

After failing to capture all the spies in South America, it was clear Hoover and the FBI had made too many mistakes. Elizebeth and her team, along with the Army and Navy, stopped sharing details with the FBI.

It was too risky, and winning the Invisible War was too important.

Elizebeth and her team monitored dozens of circuits. A circuit is a pair of radio stations sharing information.

Elizebeth cracked the codes of every radio circuit except one. But by winter 1942, she noticed circuit 3-N used a stronger than normal code. This could only mean one thing...

They are using an Enigma.

Elizebeth learned to make and break codes using paper and pencil. But cryptology was getting more advanced. New machines were invented to create codes.

The most famous machine was called Enigma.

People claimed the Enigma created unbreakable codes. It worked like a typewriter, but the Enigma replaced the real letters with coded letters from one of three wheels.

The Enigma created 16,900 alphabets—almost limitless possibilities of ciphers.

The key determined the setting of the three wheels. And the keys changed all the time. To read the code, you needed to know the key. Unless you were Elizebeth.

Elizebeth followed her methods. She stacked the messages and gathered data. She lined up the codes in columns.

Line up the messages, solve the messages, figure out the alphabet, learn the wheel, find the key.

Then, the spies made a mistake. Twenty-eight messages arrived with the same key.

Ah! They have used the same starting point. Now all we have to do is find the pattern.

She stacked them. She did a frequency count. She found the words *Bericht* (report) and *wir hören* (we hear).

We solved it! We can read every message they send.

Codebreakers in England built computers to crack the Enigma. But Elizebeth did it with a sharp pencil and her highly trained brain.

And now we know where they are!

In February 1943, Sargo and Luna were set up in Argentina. They had 42 collaborators.

They were careful. They sent only short bursts of information. They sent decoy messages with nonsense. They transmitted at different times each week. And they never repeated the same message.

But Elizebeth had cracked their code and could read every message.

This says, "We have antenna 100m long." They are planning something big. We must keep reading but don't let them know.

Elizebeth and the other intelligence officers kept the information away from Hoover so he couldn't spring the trap too early.

Sargo and Luna aren't talking about materials and machines. They are focused on politics and revolution.

Their goal was to assemble nations against the United States. They wanted to unite Argentina, Paraguay, Bolivia, Chile, pressure Uruguay and draw in Brazil. The messages showed they were working with Argentina to overthrow other governments and to plot revolutions across the continent.

Finally, they felt it was time to take action.

We know Argentina is conspiring with the Nazis. We must stop them, but we must do it without revealing that we know how to read their codes.

We also learned they are sending a man named Osmar Hellmuth to try and buy weapons.

If we capture him, we can say he revealed the plan, and keep our codebreaking a secret.

In November 1943, the British found Hellmuth on a ship in Trinidad. They took him to England. He told the British the true identities of Sargo and Luna. He also confessed that the Nazis worked in Argentina to overthrow the Bolivian government.

It was time to find Sargo and Luna.

In January 1944, Argentina ended its relationship with the Nazis. FBI agents were finally cleared to hunt down the spies.

In August 1944, they found and arrested Luna.

They continued to hunt for Sargo. He wasn't caught until April 1945. He had dyed his hair black as a disguise.

While agents worked in South America, Elizebeth had one more mission. She decoded messages sent by another spy, Velvalee Dickinson, known as the Doll Lady. The Doll Lady had been sending coded letters about Allied ship movements in exchange for money.

She's using an open code. It reads like a normal letter about a granddaughter's doll, an English doll, and family, but she means U.S. ships, a British ship, and the Japanese fleet.

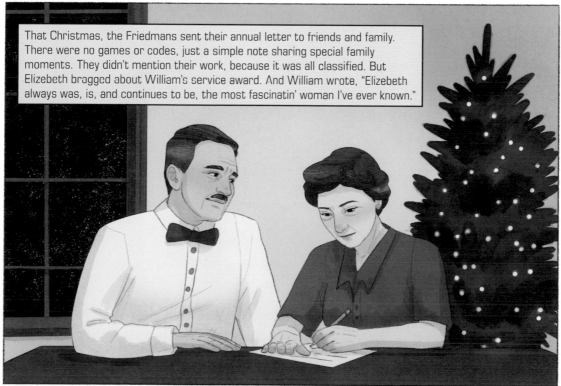

That Christmas, the Friedmans sent their annual letter to friends and family. There were no games or codes, just a simple note sharing special family moments. They didn't mention their work, because it was all classified. But Elizebeth bragged about William's service award. And William wrote, "Elizebeth always was, is, and continues to be, the most fascinatin' woman I've ever known."

At the end of the Invisible War, Elizebeth and her team had 4,000 decryptions of Nazi messages and had defeated 48 different radio circuits, including three Enigma machines.

But Elizebeth couldn't tell anyone about her work. She was sworn to secrecy. Her whole team was.

J. Edgar Hoover wasn't. In 1944, he published a story in *The American Magazine* that claimed the FBI defeated the Nazis in South America. He also made a 15-minute film called *The Battle of the United States* that also gave the FBI all the credit.

Elizebeth wrote up a technical history of her work during the war, to be used as a guide and reference for future codebreaking.

Elizebeth was done with government work. She wanted to spend time with her family and finish writing her books.

After William died, Elizebeth catalogued and indexed both of their extensive papers and records and sent them to the George Marshall Library. Everyone wanted to research William.

In 1952, the National Security Agency was established. The NSA named an auditorium after William but left her name off. Elizebeth didn't object.

When Elizebeth died in 1980, none of her obituaries even mentioned her work as a codebreaker.

But Elizebeth knew best of all that nothing stays secret for long. Researchers learned about her work. Her papers were declassified, and she is finally getting the credit and gratitude she deserved.

For Elizebeth, it was never about the spotlight.

Solving a message is the thrill of your life.

GLOSSARY

bootleg (BOOT-lehg)—unauthorized or illegal

cipher (SYE-fur)—a method of secret writing that usually involves replacing letters with other letters or numbers

circuit (SUR-kuht)—a pair of radio transmitters that share information

clandestine (klan-DEH-sten)—secret

classified (KLA-suh-fyed)—information that is restricted, secret, or private

code (KOHD)—a group of letters or symbols with special meanings used in sending messages

counterespionage (kown-tur-eh-SPEE-uh-nahj)—the activity concerned with detecting and stopping enemy spies

cryptology (krip-TAH-luh-gee)—the scientific study of writing, analyzing, and deciphering secret codes

decipher (dee-SYE-fuhr)—to decode or interpret the meaning of something

Nazi (NAHT-zee)—a member of a German fascist party controlling Germany from 1933 to 1945 under Adolf Hitler

Prohibition (pro-uh-BISH-uhn)—a period of time in U.S. history when it was illegal to sell or make alcoholic beverages like beer or wine

smuggler (SMUHG-luhr)—to take in or out of a country illegally

READ MORE

Roman, Carole P. *Spies, Code Breakers, and Secret Agents: A World War II Book for Kids.* Emeryville, CA: Rockridge Press, 2020.

Scwartz, Ella. *Can You Crack the Code?: A Fascinating History of Ciphers and Cryptography.* New York: Bloomsbury Children's Books, 2019.

Wallmark, Laurie. *Code Breaker, Spy Hunter: How Elizebeth Friedman Changed the Course of Two World Wars.* New York: Abrams Books for Young Readers, 2021.

INTERNET SITES

National Security Agency: NSA Historical Figures
nsa.gov/History/Cryptologic-History/Historical-Figures/
Historical-Figures-View/Article/1623028/elizebeth-s-
friedman/

Purdue University: Cryptology for Kids
https://www.cerias.purdue.edu/education/k-12/
teaching_resources/lessons_presentations/
cryptology.html

The International Spy Museum
spymuseum.org

ABOUT THE AUTHOR

Elizabeth Pagel-Hogan is an author and teacher from Pittsburgh, PA. She loves exploring history and science and has written over a dozen fiction and nonfiction books and graphic novels. Her books include *The Science and Technology of Leonardo da Vinci* and *Animal Allies: 15 Amazing Women in Wildlife Research*. Elizabeth lives with her family and pet schnoodle and loves board games, birding, and baking. She's a lifelong runner and avid community scientist.

ABOUT THE ILLUSTRATOR

Alisha Monnin was born and raised in rural Ohio in a small village where distance is measured by cornfields. Growing up, she was a voracious reader and daydreamed about going on magical adventures. As an adult, she still spends her days daydreaming and reading, but now her imagination is funneled into her artwork. She graduated from the Savannah College of Art and Design, and now resides in Cincinnati, Ohio, with her Manx cat named Beignet.